-gape-seed-

Editors: Ice Gayle Johnson, Jane Ormerod

Senior Editor: Brant Lyon

Junior Editor: Thomas Fucaloro

gape-seed

Copyright © 2011 by Uphook Press

Acknowledgements:

Photograph of Regie Cabico by Les Talusan

ISBN: 978-0-9799792-3-1

Library of Congress Control Number: 2011930489

First edition

Printed in the United States of America

www.greatweatherformedia.com

editors@greatweatherformedia.com

great weather for

-gape-seed-

■Uphook Press■

CONTENTS

INTRODUCTION

Whoever we are, wherever we find ourselves, we all have dreams and aspirations, high hopes and fantasies. We all want something: to achieve, to possess, be, whether one of our favorite things to do is being gay half the time (or less), or to sleep with another man's wife. We are seized by an idea, ineffable or explicit, that compels us to act. Sometimes we manage to do it, sometimes not. We face disappointment, coming to grips with a world where everything is not what it used to be, or as it ought, imagined in ways in which even the most beautiful may be too delicate, easily shorn of its wings and etherized. Our idea of life turned on its head. The Buddha might be a cigar-chomping truck driver, and gangsters go out not with a manly bang but a whimper—goodfellas become marshmallows, dropped like limp forget-me-nots. One of two separated would-be lovers lost in thought on the other side of town. Kaleidoscopic reminiscences, speculation, miscalculation, regret. Of endless fascination and invention and limitless ideals. We all sow gape seed. Even if it's only fractionalized or hyphenated, a hybrid of missing antecedents and still-to-comes.

A rock sculptor, a creator of psychedelic environments for music, fridge magnet tosser, hyper-enthused dancer that blasphemes and prays simultaneously, a snorkeler and butterfly aficionado: the poets in this, our third anthology, aspire to more than writing. Their poems broaden our vision at the same time they narrow their cynosure to a fine point, though that point may be left to the reader, for they don't preach, nor do they sit on their asses. Perhaps it's the kernel of wisdom contained in each—of lessons learned, of resilience, insight sprouting in dark places, or, conversely, the stuff of not knowing—that makes you want to hold them in your chest pocket for safekeeping. We invite you to take them out to read aloud, for, as in our previous anthologies, we appreciate the aural experience of a poem, and continue to dedicate ourselves to supporting a community of poets who enjoy publicly performing their work.

We are especially proud to present the work of high-reaching slam master and spoken word artist, Regie Cabico, who also shares his views on the current scene, its expectations, shortcomings and grand successes, the up- and downside of competition, rigors of performance, and the need for a water bottle at the ready.

These poems whisper or shout. Whoever you are, wherever you are, whoever you're with or without, may they plant something in you.

Here's the germ. ■

SOMEWHERE

Somewhere my real father is eating an egg sandwich
Under a lamppost in the rain.
He's thinking about high-ceilinged rooms.
He's thinking about God and mathematics.
He's thinking about the heightening of his own circumstances.
He's thinking of ways to perceive things in a wider way.
His leather satchel is full of pay stubs and dead beetles
And when he makes love nights he does it clumsily
Arms splayed everywhere like a convulsing mantis.
And he's thinking again about rainy afternoons in 1847
His pants are full of gouges and holes.
He had a dream last night of a man pushing another man
Off a roof.
Somewhere he's eating Chinese food in the near future.
Somewhere a small dog is following him into a video arcade.
If you look closely at his handwriting
You'll notice that the g's look like nooses.

KELLY POWELL

WHAT IF BUDDHA WAS A MOVING MAN?

The one driving the truck smoking
a cigar and belching, showing up
drunk and breaking the credenza.

Not the spiritual guy writing the great
American novel about the road, the work,
the hardship toil, the part-time teacher
with the keen intellect, tortured artist
sex appeal and heart of gold.

What if his wife has just left him?

And his kids hate him and he goes home
to a rented room and gets drunk
and watches porn, suicidal every night
and he gets pissed off.

What if he tells the boss to go fuck himself?

And the boss tells him he's had enough
That he better straighten his sorry ass out
and this is his last chance
or he has to hit the highway
and he has rent to pay and child support
and his mother, friend and dog has just died.

What if he wrecks the truck?

Not in a superficial way. In a way
that hurts people, throws a tractor
trailer over a bridge killing people,
leaving a trail of destruction.

What if he's the driver, the writer,
the boss, the wife, the kids, the mother
the people he killed, the friend
and the dog?

Then he'll almost be the Buddha.

What if he gets back in the truck
and tells people his story, helps
them on their journey?

Then he'll almost be the Buddha.

What if he learns to live and laugh
and love again and it happens
all over again?

Then he'll be himself.

What if he gets back in the truck
and tells people his story, helps
them on their journey and
the same things keep happening
over and over and he keeps

getting back in the truck and tells
people his story and helps them
on their journey and he keeps
crashing and getting back up
and crashing and loving and
laughing and getting back up
and it keeps happening over
and over and over?

Then he'll be everyone, himself
and the Buddha and he'll
be smoking a cigar, swearing
driving the truck.

WHAT HAPPENS WHEN YOU SUPERSIZE MY HAPPY KITTEN AND UNICORN TIME WITH ZOMBIES?

I am currently immersing myself
in all things zombie, to educate myself
on the subtle nuances.
Do these pants make me look emo?
Zombie emo?
My kitten, Resin-tastic, loves to bring me
to that dark, hopeless time of golf-playing
kitties in the Antarctic, where the skies
were always blue, and every day
was Happy Kitten and Unicorn Time—
in other words, the 70's.
What do you get when you cross
Happy Kitten and Unicorn Time
with Zombies?—Oscar Wilde balls
on Jared from Subway.
Jared-from-Subway-WE-GET-IT-ALREADY-STFU
told TMZ, "MC Hammer tried restricting my
Nintendo time, but a duck divided by a Kitten Cannon
shooting Super Sled Kitten Racing
out of water fairy butt
was a good way of letting him know
that when you play Slayer's 1986
thrash metal classic Reign in Blood
backwards you hear 'Step aside,
President Johnson, it's my turn to brain-fuck.'"

What are your three favorite
things to do?
Mine are being gay 43% of the time
white >43%, and taking
the path less traveled
(but someone less gay else can have
the credit for that).
Hopefully, by the time I retire,
I'll only have puppies and kittens
to take care of, but right now I got
ninety-nine problems, and a bitch ain't one.
Wait—I got ninety-nine problems
and they're all bitches.

THANKS TO EVERY AXE THAT BROKE MY HEART

Dead Tony told me
"every 5 years I'd look back & think
'fuck I was an asshole then,' until
I finally realized that means I'm
most likely an asshole
now"

& I look back on every midnight lamentation
& I relive every moment bemoaned
& every scab-ripping rail toss turn
I take back the curses & pleas
& thank you each and every
for doing what I hadn't the balls to do
but needed desperate doing
molt my walls
of calcified dreams
& ossified fears
& inadequacies so internalized they acted inherent

& I could crab-like grow
past the point of safe
to soft-shelled sensate
& scuttle across the sand
to settle here

R. YURMAN

A MEDITATION ON PLEASURE

An old man daydreams
in the sun of dark
nipples against his tongue

the naked innocence
of a lover's neck bent over him
mouth and lips obscured

skin of hips and thighs
electric under his fingertips
the softest most delicate velvet

and feels the laughter rise in him.

He rocks his chair
with the joy of it
and the rocking sustains him.

WAKE

I. The Third Time Castro Died

before being resurrected, eternal
anti-Christ, by the island media,
the Miami stations reported *it could be*,
Perez Hilton blogged with assurance

and Ileana Ros-Lehtinen perfected
speeches about *exilio* and freedom
while sipping *cortaditos* at Versailles.

Before the doubled police
force tightened security, we laid
in supplies as if for a hurricane
party: limes, mint, all the makings

for *mojitos*. The gas stove
stood at the ready, the pots
and pans for ad hoc feasts.

Before today there were rafts
of raw words on the currents,
fish to be hooked and strung
together. When bitter sugar

finally does become sweet,
what will be left for the poets
to drink or eat?

II. At Kelly's Landing

after the funeral of a friend
who died from stomach cancer,
it was the season of soft shells
when lobsters can't mate or grow

unless they molt, and waitresses
delivered plates of twins to lovers
who could rip them apart with hands.

We appeased ourselves by dunking
the fragile bellies of steamers
into broth, then butter, half-listening
to the ambient, unmetered verse

of a roomful of discarded
exoskeletons as we awaited
our Darwinian orders.

III. Driving Wine Country

on the morning the death of Julia Child
was announced with the solemnity
of a young daughter offering her mother
a taste of gravelly, homemade mud cakes,

heading up-valley on the St. Helena Highway
where the vines sprout offspring like a woman
filled to rupture with multiple births,

Dry Creek behind me and Calistoga
with its couples' mud baths and hot
stone therapy ahead, directions
inarguable as clarified butter, I thought

about the woman who had read the night
before about trying to quit the habit
of verse and elusive prosody,

against a backdrop of foliage black-eyed
by the double fists of cabernet
and dusk, in front of a natural pool
the hue of decaffeinated iced tea,

who later joked about walking across water
because really, if you can make people
laugh with poetry the power is yours,

and I accelerated through old vine zinfandels
and Prohibition-era blocks of pinot noir,
head-trained like hippies and thickened
by the effort of producing for so many years,

and in some vineyards the silver flags, planted
to deter birds, flashed emergency, and in others,
with bright-eyed efficiency, they simply effervesced.

CAN SAFETY MATCHES MAKE US SAFE?

You read the tiny cardboard book before
you scratch the strip under *Augie's New Pizza*
on the back of *MIA: We still don't know*
(and isn't that the truth?). *Earn college
credit at home*, taking tests on a screen
being screened. *Bad credit? We can help.*
Remember to *close cover before striking*
or go out on strike /// three strikes: you're out
of the fire into a plastic frying pan, teflon
on electric glowing rings—not like when
your phone rings and someone tells you
what you know you don't want to know.

CHARLENE MONAHAN SPEAREN

UNKNOWN ZONE

Glossary: abnormal, chronic, bipolar, schizoid, manic, traumatized, trigger, man your guns

='s

Loopy: looped, lollygags way too much, limbo, lethargic, lays flat and lines up late nights

='s

Anxiety: run forward, run backward, running in place, I believe I want to, no, I know I can fly

='s

Nervous Disorder: hearing voices, bound-up, dancing down stage for you, him, her, them, upstaging the one in the mirror

='s

Get another hit: rag doll, head up, head turns, head droops, he pushes pills, I pop two, three, four

='s

Undone

='s

Another breakdown, breakup, break out, break into too many pieces

='s

Walking emotional balance beams, emotional train wreck, tossed further and further into the air.

EXIT

TODD ANDERSON

22 CANDLES AND IT'S STILL DARK OUT

I turned 22
    on an empty Brooklyn rooftop
    under an empty sky

I turned 7
    wearing a paper crown
        and swinging a wooden sword
    in a backyard kingdom where I
        got to choose all the citizens

I turned 12
    in a mini-van bound for Chicago
        next to my dog,
            drugged with Benadryl
  My parents bought me a video game
        but I didn't have a house
        to play it in

I turned 22
    Searching for the symbolism
        that's supposed to hang on birthdays
        like Christmas lights

I turned 16
    paddling down a flooded Canadian river
        We ate powdered cake that night
        with powdered frosting

I turned 18
        smoking cheap cigars
                flipping through Penthouse
                        and scratching lotto tickets
            in the parking lot
                outside of the Seven-Eleven

I turned 22
        Replaying the dusty VHS tape of my life story
        Remembering as hard as I could
        what it was like
        to turn 7
        12
        16
        18

I turned 20
        At a shitty diner called Kappy's,
                which we lovingly dubbed "Krappy's",
      eating a slice of inedibly old birthday cake
            while the oldest
                    ugliest
          waitress you can imagine
              sang the worst
          rendition of Happy Birthday
             you can imagine
          My friends sung at first,
                then faded out of earshot
          to avoid going down with the ship

I turned 21
        Chugging the remains of a Jameson bottle
                while everyone hugged me,
        then crying against her chest
                an hour later;
        something I wondered
                if her boyfriend ever did
        She should've known better
        than to invite me into her bed
        that night

        For my birthday present
                she bought me a drink
        called a "Blowjob"
                I didn't think it was funny

I turned 22
        on an empty Brooklyn rooftop
                under an empty sky
        with no more locks on the chastity belt of the world
                A year when life means what you want it to,
        and empty is another word for waiting

LABOR

The nightwatch performs its usual now-you-see-it-now-you-don'ts in the dormitories.
  André Breton

A stain is an echo of what may not be seen—
This one, dark and muddy
or bloody like spilled wine
recalls a certain circle of heavy breathing
in the still silent center of which something suddenly moves.

That cry which resounds builds a wall in a field
that is fenced
by the far face of flowers.

And when the back is curved, an archer's tensed bow,
and the hands are cuffed securely,
then a light clicks off in the other room—
that's all.

A light clicks off in the other room   and work is done.

(February 24, 1982 / January 28, 2007)

CHRISTOPHER LUNA

THE AUTOBIOGRAPHY OF CHRISTOPHER'S INNER EAR

Believe it or not, it began with the scream of a tiny man who lived inside my pillow, shouting messages my young ears may not have been ready to hear. At first it frightened me, but as I grew, it left me and was replaced with a softer, interior suggestion. A whisper so quiet that it was often overwhelmed by the yelping machinery of my monkey mind.

Later still I discovered that one ignores this whisper at one's peril. Missing it, or worse, disregarding it, could send you careening wildly off the path. Your heart could break. You might lose everything.

You might even find yourself on the other side of the world, cut off from family, friends, and any sense of who you are, and what it means.

After completion, begin again.

I have always found it difficult to stop myself from picking at the scab, peeling it away. I want to understand where it came from, want to enter the wound, swim around in the pool of new cells forming. Easier to pick at it than to forgive. Easier than taking responsibility. Anger becomes an old friend. Self-pity flattens me, turns me into That Guy, the one who bores the shit out of everyone, cornering unsuspecting partygoers to rant about some ancient slight.

There are more and less accurate descriptions of the veins on the back of her hand, the contours of each chamber of her heart. All inadequate to describe what emanates forth through the breastbone, skin, and hair to press against the chest of her lover. Pulls him close, all too aware that this warmth is fleeting, that this moment is eager to flutter away, that soon enough he and she and you and we will all be gone.

Not enough. Love renders us childlike, beseeching: "Stay!" Wailing for more: "Please. I'll do *anything*!"

"Everything grows by rubbing together"
Michael McClure

My hunger cannot be satiated. I might eat everything, so it is definitely better that this is not socially acceptable. She opens her eyes and I fall in.

Lose
my self.
Not
complaining.
Drink it in.
Could mean trouble.
Trouble all around.

Namaste,
fiery reflection.
You are right.
So right.
Always.

Unspooling forth from the heart which stubbornly regenerates despite innumerable scorching incidents. We are all ash, but we are also the seed which takes root, the shoot that stretches green tendrils toward the sky, unafraid of black clouds heavy with foreboding regret. Unleash your worst. Drench me in it. Left my skin behind long ago. Exposed myself to the flame of indiscretion, torture, and betrayal. The endless searing of your fear passed on no—no, jammed down my throat. Keep your wounds to yourself. I can only take so much before I will need to cloak myself in that thin layer of protection once again. Before I will rise to speak in my own voice. Before I will let it go, shut the door.

I used to train caterpillars, coach them through every moment of their pupal journey. Self-righteous. Justified in resenting them for spreading their wings and flying away from me. Spent years struggling to figure out where I went wrong, how I could guarantee a different outcome.

Now I just give.

Now I just watch, listen, try to learn what I can.

CROSS WORDS

Across:

1   Dear _____, letter

6   Some Like It _____

12   A volcano erupts in Italy and you ask me if I still love you

19   Romeo and Juliet

43   Plumlike is not a plum; nothing has ever depended on a plum

57   Simile is not a substitute for your breath on my neck

70   Is finer more exquisite?

Down:

3   Sexton anagram: rats live on no evil _____ (with –"crossed"
    and 19-across)

8   Neither oleo nor oleander are related to this crème-filled
    sandwich cookie

13   Swit of "M*A*S*H" had lips swifter than _____

29 I _____ you, every day

33 Alpha-numeric password strength is weak, please create a new password

50 Count the days (that I'm gone) 1, 2 , 3, _____

61 Even the sharpest metaphor is aware of its own limitations

79 For answers, call _____

FIRST OF THE MONTH

life was a journey you were
a hobo in my heart life went
faster than fast—earth went
spinning so swell so colorful
so swell so swell so swell &
true—we walked down hudson
st arm in arm we went dizzy
down the avenue my heart
was a silver dollar in your
hand you tossed it over the
river like george washington
my heart was a guinea pig
your heart was a guinea pig
too you stuck a needle in it
the lime trees were in bloom
the sky was made of cotton candy
yes the carnival had come to town
we were pretty as a dining room in
the country painted by pierre bonnard
jacques cousteau went for a nice cool dive
in our ice blue waters your skin was perfect
my skin was perfect—then you stabbed
your fist through the canvas of our
life—everything falls apart you
sd everything comes back
together again—but not us

not us—this is new york you sd
anything can happen—you sd
i'll do anything you want baby
—you touched me i came apart
but that was only temporary—
no man you just don't get it—
you cannot put this old humpty
dump back together it's broke
down can't fix it that's the sum &
total of it—when i'm wrong
i'm right you sd for a long
time i believed that—
when you're wrong
you refuse to fight you sd
at least you got that right—
i keep things to myself
like the first time you gave me
a bloody lip like all the times
i propped you up &
carried you home—
here's a fact—the melting pot
stops here—at the end of your fist,
you prick—i don't care if you are
the original survivor—ready for
anything the world can throw
at you—a man like you—
if you want you can
skyscrape heaven—

well ok babe but not with
me—this is the new me in
new york city—after the fall
pal—get up tear off your clothes—
say let me fuck you baby—
hard as you are you're
not hard enough for that—
not no more not in your dreams—
day by day mayday by mayday
you made that impossible—
over & done—first of
the month rent due—
fifteenth round—
baby what you
going to do—
KO the sky?

LIZA WOLSKY

WHAT THE MOUTH DOES

What the mouth does
is
a rose that chooses to

fold its petals into the green area of
shuttered
and shattered falling
to touch the ground
lips first
metallic blood
slipping
against the
teeth
of
desire.

Falling follows chasing.

Open to inhale the caustic
flow
of
what we never thought of.

Stopping follows chasing.

A cloud
will pass between our teeth,

I can already feel
the soft
spin of it
touching against
the bony surfaces.
A sweet reminiscent candy
that makes my bones hurt
licking.

Licking follows chasing.
What follows stopping?

Stopping follows falling
Falling follows chasing.

I make sounds,
and your face changes when you hear them.
How close can I get to
making the face that I want?

Uphook Press checks in with award-winning poet and spoken word pioneer, Regie Cabico

Olfactory, Oratorical, and Hydrated
AN INTERVIEW WITH REGIE CABICO

What's new with Regie Cabico?

Since I left New York City in 2006, I have relocated to Washington DC, and have performed throughout Canada and England. I love New York. You can't *not* write in the city, but I feel being there for almost two decades sometimes puts you in a bubble. I still continue to teach at New York's Bellevue Hospital, have been involved with The Howl Festival, and work with Urban Word NYC. I am still single and thriving in the rapidly growing spoken word community here in DC.

Stick your finger in the wind. Where is performance poetry headed nowadays? Where would you like to see it go?

Performance poetry is fast, unpredictable, and still underground. I would love to see American Theater and the performance poetry/slam/ spoken word community intersect. Our political theater is found in spoken word poetry. I like to think of a slam poem as a three-minute play, a Broadway showstopper. I wish poets would think out of the box regarding their topics—I'm always on the lookout for performance poems that are out of the box. I encourage poets to be in touch with their sense of humor. I know a wonderful performance poet in Canada who has a really intense delivery and has poems about cancer that are just as heavy. I encouraged her to write a poem about breakfast. Especially in the slam, poets are writing with their "high stakes and up-against-the wall" drama. I'd like to see more gleeful and upbeat, original slam poems. Also, the internet is the biggest promoter of performance poetry, but I do hope people still come to the real live cafe experience of a poet.

There's a muzzy line between spoken word and poetry—or is there? Should there be?

I think there definitely is a "muzzy" line. I can write a really terse economic slam poem but if you read it, it would not give you the choreography and vocals that accompany it. My "Midlife Crisis of the Olfactory Kind" is a spoken word poem developed over time in front of several audiences. I remember doing a show in Montreal and asking for the recording so I could transcribe parts that were improvised in the reading. I have never written a poem like that. In general, I like slam performance poems to work "on the page"—full of imagery, poetic devices, a poem framed with a beginning, middle, and end. Storytelling, however, is a genre that does need to work well on the page. Like a standard play. The battle is won in the performance. I am more open to stories that are not on the page; however I do hope the storyteller can deliver the story with great oratorical skill.

From what other art forms do you draw inspiration?

Musical theater, show tunes, standards, Stephen Sondheim, singer songwriters, pandora.com, the Museum of Modern Art gift shop catalog, astrobarry.com, Ingrid Michaelson, sangria bars, gay bath houses, independent cinema, pasta sauces, Paranormal State, a broken heart, doubt, Hindu temples, teaching at-risk youth, The New York Neo-Futurists.

When you first began slamming in the early '90s you were a maverick amid a predominantly macho heterosexist milieu. When and how did it become alright for you to honestly express yourself as (as you've been called) "the Lady Gaga of Poetry"?

If I was going to be judged on stage, I had to be honest with myself. With my identity as a queer Filipino-American guy. I was obsessed with racial stereotyping and the invisibility of queer Asian men/ experience in the media. As an actor, I was never Asian enough for the playwright or director's concept. If I was a maverick, or a shock of the new, it's because I was the poster child of an East Coast Filipino-American migration and an artist rising from the devastation of AIDS. I still believe that AIDS left a huge generation gap and a lack of mentorship in the '90s. I feel that the younger generation of artists have bonded closely with my work. I am a queer Asian model for a talented collection of Asian-American spoken word poets. This younger group keeps me on my feet and in shape. I want to be relevant not because of what I did but because I am saying things that are vital to me now. It has taken me a long time to discover Regie Cabico, as the forty-year-old as opposed to the angry twenty-year-old that drove my initial slam poems at the Nuyorican Poets Cafe. If I have anything that is Lady Gaga, it's that I hope to give riveting performances where the content is real and risky. There needs to be some kind of danger in the reading—otherwise, what's the point?! We have the ability to push the envelope. Whenever I perform, I gauge the crowd and figure out a set that will drive the audience to the edge—how "gay" can I get with this crowd? But more importantly, what do they need to hear and what do I have to say? This is always a battle with performing poets.

Is there any subject you won't write about? As you've gotten older has that changed?

It's been hard to write about my teaching at Bellevue Hospital. I have been doing it for over a decade. It's a job that keeps me humble and childlike. My poems have gotten so more and more audacious that I don't feel like reading them, or sometimes I get embarrassed by my own foibles of romantic doubt.

Winner of the National Poetry slam several years, you should know: What's the upside/downside of poetry as competition? What do you advise the aspiring poets you coach?

There is a Canadian book that came out this year, *The Spoken Word Workbook* edited by Sheri-D Wilson, with an essay of mine about writing, history, and performance which you might want to check out. Regarding the poetry slam, it's an imperfect beast. It brings out the Black Swan from the poet and sucks the duende from your soul. That said, the slam is one of the most important literary and theatrical inventions of the 20th century. Starting in the late '80s (by

Chicago construction worker-poet, Marc Smith) at the peak of the performance art movement, in the aftermath of AIDS and the rise of multicultural publishing, poetry slam was a soapbox for anyone there to wow, cajole, and incite an audience. You have three minutes to use language to say something without using props, musical accompaniment, or costumes.

The downside to this is what wins; writing alone will not win it. So many times the delivery and the performance pyrotechnics win. I'd like to believe that passion wins, but that doesn't happen. The upside to poetry as competition is the way the audience will be at the edge of their seats, mouth open, clinging to every word. When I'm under the gun I perform in a way that I don't normally. I have started to slam again. There is a growing homophobic and misogynistic vibe throughout some open mics in Washington DC. The Christian hip hop/spoken word movement is also pervasive. I started a queer open mic called SPARKLE at Busboys & Poets to counteract the hate and to create a forum where queer poets can speak. In my old age I am still shocked by the censorship and hate that exists. I slammed in 1993 because people of color, women, and queer poets were embraced. And now I see that these poets are attacked.

I started slamming again to change the sound and challenge the themes, and to create an intergenerational community in Washington DC. Also, as a slam coach, advisor, and teacher it was important for me to put myself in the slam so I could be empathetic and to see that my input wasn't dated. I made it to finals but the night of competition my voice went out; I had a fever, and I totally bombed (tour exhaustion).

I was happy that I found something to say but I also learned how important it is for performing poets to stay healthy, hydrated and focused like an athlete. The main point is, WHAT DO YOU WANT TO SAY? WHAT IS YOUR MESSAGE? At the end of the day, the scores should not matter, so long as you have said what you wanted to say. I also believe that the universe had a hand in me not making the DC slam team, and I'll still try to find the time to slam because developing the slam poems or the poems that do well in slam (I cannot write slam poems consciously—in eighteen years of writing, I only have maybe eight slam poems) are the poems that keep me gigging, going, and gigaloing.

REGIE CABICO slammed through the '90s, first winning the Nuyorican Poets Café Grand Slam in 1993, then on to take top prizes in the National Poetry Slams, and appearing in two seasons of HBO's Def Poetry Jam. His publications span over thirty anthologies, including *Aloud: Voices from the Nuyorican Poets Café*, *Spoken Word Revolution*, and *The Outlaw Bible of American Poetry*. Numerous awards honor his work in poetry and performance, theatre, and teaching: a 2008 grant from The Ford Foundation, three New York Foundation for the Arts Fellowships for Poetry and Multidisciplinary Performance, Larry Neal Awards for Poetry in 2007 and 2008, a DC Commission for the Arts Poetry Fellowship, and the 2006 Writers for Writers Award from Poets & Writers for his work teaching at-risk youth at New York's Bellevue Hospital. He has been a faculty member of Banff's Spoken Word Program and at Kundiman, and artist in residence at NYU's Asian Pacific American Studies Program and Deanza College.

As a theatre artist, he has directed plays, received three New York Innovative Theatre Award Nominations for work in *Too Much Light Makes the Baby Go Blind*, including a Best Performance Art Production award in 2006. Regie's plays have been produced at the Humana Theatre Festival; his latest, *Unbuckled*, a solo play, has been presented at Lincoln Center. Longtime curator of Composer's Collaborative's Non Sequitir Series, he has otherwise performed at Kennedy Center Play Lab, Joe's Pub, La MaMa, The Kitchen, Dixon Place, and many major festivals. He is Youth Program Coordinator for Split This Rock Poetry Festival, artistic director of Sol & Soul, co-founder of the Asian American performance series SULU DC, and co-director of Capturing Fire: A Queer Spoken Word Summit. Regie is named in *BUST* magazine's list of *100 Men We Love*.

REGIE CABICO

A MIDLIFE CRISIS OF THE OLFACTORY KIND

When I was five, I smelled like a pile of hearts
being poured into a tin man.

My ex-boyfriend smells like salmon and vitamins.
His boyfriend smells like kitty litter.
Together they smell like an animal rescue.

My ex-boyfriend told me that my crotch
smelled like Bea Arthur's dentures. Bea Arthur
in *The Golden Girls* or Bea Arthur in *Futurama*?

My most recent fling happened in a bar that smelled like Neverland.
The Fling smelled like a leotard with holes.
The Fling showed me his penis on his iPhone.

I know technology means you get things right away
but that's just too immediate.

I ran into the mens' room and photographed my penis.
I came out and showed him my penis on the cell phone
and he pulled out his phone

and we were rubbing our cell phones together.
It smelled like a new kind of safe sex.

It smelled like AOL dial up internet…It smelled like passenger
pigeons flying South…No, it smelled
smoke signals fading into a bitch slap of thunder…
It smelled like the shake weight…

I recently had sex with a 20 year old
so that makes me a cougar. A gay cougar.
No, a jaguar. Better yet, a faguar.

Faguars smell like deep fried twinkies
and Demi Moore's dildo.

I want to wash the scent of my Muse. He lives
in San Francisco and when he has sex with his boyfriend
they smell like a box of Dunkin' Donut munchkins.

I just want to fall in a Merchant Ivory still,
roll with a stable boy
till we smell like sweet hay…

When I went back to The Neverland Bar,
a hobbit offered to suck my dick.

I turned around and said, "That is the nicest thing
anyone has ever said to me!" His offer smelled
a thousand pokes on Facebook
and an episode of Extreme Home Makeover.

I explained to him, I don't want a boyfriend.
I just want to have sex with a guy on a regular basis
whose name I know.

That smells like getting rid of Republicans
one blowjob at a time.

VICTORIA LYNNE McCOY

WHAT SHE CANNOT KNOW WHILE WAITING FOR HER DATE OUTSIDE THE GUGGENHEIM AS A FEBRUARY BLIZZARD WAGES WAR ON THE HOLE IN THE MIDDLE FINGER OF HER RIGHT GLOVE

Tomorrow, there will be a girl
on the kaleidoscope side
of Brooklyn losing herself
in the puzzle-piece mouth
of a man and somewhere
a man at the bruised end
of the City is already
building altars to the stained-
glass collision of a girl.

NANCY CAROL MOODY

DREAMSCAPE IN ADVANCE OF THE AFTERLIFE

After the severance, the head
bobbles among the others,
the newly rubbed skulls gleaming
like worry stones, gold
not yet pliered from the teeth.

When hope is the only nugget
we've been left, we marry
the craquelure, snap
extraneous digits from the webbed
yawns of our offsprung children.
The goats in the pasture
nibble away the nummy bits, hardsell
the gristle to the ovines next door.

Don't stew about what to tell
the neighbors: they scalped
those tickets to this listing ship,
where shuffleboard's played with tics
and noggins, and the headwaiter
in the Captain's Lounge
breaks out the umbrellas
when brainstorms are forecast
for Saturday night.

These days we mate for corpulence.
And some fat around the midsection
is not at all what I'm talking about.

You know that. Look
at your fingernails, the moons
slurried over with hardener and gloss,
seven minutes in a timered capsule
all the sun you think
you're ever going to need.

Upping-the-ante
is the new nostalgia. I'll see
your melancholy, raise you a rope.

MEANWHILE NOVA, 2

because this is the stuff of life:
this is the stuff of not knowing (where to
place the foot that is the next step,
where to unlatch with keys diaries and
doors kept (behind pillows pours logic
and reasons and things you will never
claim to have seen) she said, a girl so still and
tall that small never knew her, never knew
the speck upon which her universe pulsed)

GABRIELLA RADUJKO

GEORGIA, OVER THERE

I've got the keys, you see
the keys
to your apartment
I'm the landlord you see
with the keys

Don't want the details
of your life, you see,
but I got the keys

It's not clear when you say Georgia
It's not the state, but Georgia, like Tbilisi
Now Western Union's connecting me with you
and Georgia, but it's not Atlanta

Can't understand why you didn't just send a check
through the U. S. postal service
Cause you're in Georgia, not the state, I come to learn, but the country

Off to Pathmark to cash your rental check
You've paid fifty bucks in late fees
Cause you're in Georgia, not the state
but the country Georgia
not Atlanta
but Tbilisi

Old timer, helping your mother in Georgia,
not Atlanta, but Tbilisi
I'm not in the business of collecting late fees
I'm in the business of collecting rent
You say the money's there, I know
but you tax me with Georgia, Tbilisi, not Atlanta

Don't want the late charge, just the rent
for the apartment that I rent you,
just that, no more

Don't care about the mountain of clothes in your dining room
don't care about your Mom, really I don't, it's your Mom, your Tbilisi,
Got my own Tbilisi, here, with kids that don't have college loans
because that was my gift, my gift, my gift,
my twenties, my thirties, my forties

Don't care 'bout your mom in Tbilisi
cannot care 'bout your Mom in Tbilisi
I'm just your landlord, you see
… and thank you for your note of thanks
For saying "thank you it's been nice"
It's nice, your note, but when are you moving out?

RYAN BUYNAK

SYMPHONY ASLEEP THROUGH THIS HOLY CANNON DUKE

sing.
sick queen.
ten things.
weak end wednesdays.
three hundred and sixty five.
without numbers.

"I skipped a Turkish dinner for this."

you be me for a bit and I'll be your dumb skull, romantic at best.

over.
asleep.
holy.
yours.

"I write poems like Paul Westerberg wrote songs."

have you ever apologized twice?

Certainly.
in red.
or maroon.
or death.

"I write poems like Sidney Offit rides the crosstown bus."

everyday.
loud.
lit.
metaphorical.
pistol and knife.
windows.
hammers.
legs.
symphony.

a hole in the drapes.

ELIEL LUCERO

HOW AN UPRIGHT BASS BECAME A MACHETE
after Charles Mingus

It begins with the fingers stroking their way through the strings
the way the blind discover new countries.

The left hand making creases on its fingers
holding the strings tight on the neck.

The right hand fondling the strings below the chest,
each stroke fingered pluck, a new reason to resist.

The player's eyes are closed but the bass is wide alert.
Now the overture is done.

The strings begin to wrap around the fingers.
The neck becomes a wooden handle with two rusty nails.

The chest begins in a narrow expanding
into the navel breaking ground for the authority of the hips.

Steal now.
Cold hungry steal, with an edge sharp enough to cut shackles in one slice.

Its music is still low, pounding and heavy.
The bass-man is upset,

Pounds harder
Now he's angry

Pound pound pound
His face is red

Pound pound pound
His veins hard like sugar cane

Pound pound pound
His bare feet are swollen but he feels no ground

Pound Pound Pound
He runs with fury lifting up his bass

Slice. The first cut head rolls on a grass field.
Dead eyes search for some foreign sky.

Now there are trumpets screaming with him.
There is a drum, a piano and even a tambourine,

all sharp and furious.
The bass man cuts through another neck.

The trumpet blows head off shoulders, spine attached,
dragging a green heart, leaving torso standing in terror.

Now the keys are stomping craters
the drummer is crushing heads

With each crush another machete is raised
for every plantation new machetes are forged.

Tested on skulls holding receipts,
as if paper can guarantee ownership over flesh and fury.

The band is in full massacre.
When asking for freedom does not work,

the blade negotiates.
From the North the machetes made bloody of Saint-Domingue,

bare feet march south as new blades point to some heaven
and catch the sun before staining the ground crimson.

Fight. Pound.
Slice. Blood.

fight, pound, slice, blood,
fightpoundsliceblood

Faster and faster as the horn fills the island with rage and hope.
The song repeats and goes on for thirteen years

The Bass-man is pensive, low
never quiet, as if retelling the story to a new nation

He plucks and digs.
Washes blood and digs.

Louder.
Digs.

This is where he begins to play again.
The same pound he played in the beginning

A little happier now.
In celebration now.

The same notes and chords as a reminder.
Horns, keys and drums are louder.

With no fury but louder.
In jubilee and louder.

Retelling the story with the bass-man.
Making sure no one forgets.

Although they've stopped
I can never get over the thump slice pound and blood.

I never forget how revolution began with a blade,
how Mingus tells the story of the upright bass that became a
machete.

J. CROUSE

SO

So as in an is an as it
Is another of an is of
Any other of an in an
If an any of an is an

In an is an as an in an
Is an if an of another
Is an in an of an as an
Any of another of an

Is an is as in an is it
Is of in another of an
If an in of is of in it
Is an is of as an either

Is a way of even in an
Is of in an either of an
Other of an is an is it
Is an if an any of an

Any in another of an
In an in of is an as it
Either is another is an
Ever is an of an as an

64

Is an in an is again an
Is along an any in an
Any in another is an
Any other of an in an

Is of all an is an is it
In along an in an either
Is of it an in again an
In an in among an if an

If an is of is an else an
Is of any of another
In an is of ever is an
Of about another is an

Is about an if an is an
Is an if an any other
Is an if an in along an
If an is among an is an

Is an in an if again an
Even if an in an all an
In an is an in an on an
In again an of enough an

GOOGLING A PRESENT PARTICIPLE

to revolve at the end of a stick
just a memory from long ago   sitting with friends on the curb
a method where you alter the direction of every other pallet
using two contrasting colors
make designs on your glass beads

this thing where when she gets excited she stands
on her back feet and waves her front paws in the air
often going in different directions
it involves using a artificial like windmill head
on the tail

for people who like:
gifts
unique
baby
handmade
etsy
artful
delicate
mobile
motion
pinwheels

the act of turning a multiple-screw ship within a minimum radius
by having some engines going forward and others going in reverse

a whole section of road   covered in sod
with pinwheels stuck in it

after importing into dsp and putting into track 1 the application
will freeze when trying to play in the viewer and when they do work
most of the video   is black and only the
last portion of the video will play

for people who like:
anthropologie
cotton
flowers
intimates
jersey
lingerie
pattern
pinkerton
underwear

an alternative or more manly term for pirouette?
when a male is wheeling (working; flirting; gaming; playing) a girl
on a blackberry, through pinning

the act of twirling your boner out the sun roof of a moving vehicle
to elicit interest from the opposite sex

a sexual position where the female is in a handstand and the male
performs oral sex then she switches to a standing position

and sexual intercourse begins alternating between the two
usually for the more active sexual couple
looking for a real work out

a unfortunate side effect of being rather ill   and your body evacuates
from both exits
a futile grab for balance   into a dark space that smelled strongly
of cinnamon

pinwheeling

KUDOS FOR YOU

I'd throw kudos if I had any to throw,
or any right to throw them.

When I didn't like the food on my plate,
my mother would say, *You don't know what's good.*

Why didn't she just give me a cookie?

I still don't know what's good.

Has my body rebelled, or are you really bad at eating pussy?
It didn't used to take much.
Or maybe I didn't know it was bad, so it was good.

I envy the girl in yellow who is too stupid to know she is stupid.
Probably her pussy likes everybody, an excellent state of affairs.

I dream of non-discretionary nights, the magic of "last call"
transforming everyone into possibility, no need to remember
encounters, tomorrow's bar turned you back into strangers.

I'd throw kudos if I knew how you tasted, or your dog's name,
or your shoe size, or your favorite nightmare, or what you were doing
the first time you heard the Ramones.

I'd throw kudos if you remembered to go left
without being told.

I'd throw kudos if I knew
what was good.

WOE BE GALL

woe be gall

and woe be the urgent horse damp flank
woe be he whose love is sorrow and believes the angels watch him
from their burning sphere
he heard it from a psychic half-deaf and drunk over a lunch
held secret from his wife his work pants hid
a scar on his calf   trembling hands
the bowls in giddy swells as she stabled her arms upon the
table

do you know who watches you

this was a painting in his father's velvet den
Japanese prayer card
a sense of sword he knew his namesake

badkneed into October steam soba veined

he faithed most anything, with a clovey sense of optimism
and rye
it would return and pet his leg
a tree

woe be he who believes the world will soften with age

woe be the horse's eyes in the stomach of man trudging to an
empty field
to be modest before stones   incomplete
         woe
woe woe and woe be he who believes the angels hold him as the
crows crawl down

SONGS CALLED MEMORIES THAT YOU WON'T STOP ME FROM
CONSUMING

When I'm at a party
And someone points
To the weed and booze
While asking what's my poison

I look at them
And ask
Which is your religion

And before they answer
I tell them
My poison
My religion
Is my family

Because
No venom
Is as consuming
As blood

And it is with this
Blind love
This mute addiction
That I comprehend
Your piety

Mom
Dad

You are my shepherd
And I
Your lost sheep
Do not forsake me
For I am the image
Of your tenderness

And don't take this as prayer
Because prayer is not prayer
It's begging
Lowly and foul

So when I'm at a party
And I've already had
Five shots of my father

I tell them
Hugging your mother
Because Dad doesn't know how
Is prayer

I tell them
Realizing your brother
Isn't a hero anymore
Is prayer

I tell them
To watch the stove
Because Mom's memory
Is burning like the gas
It's a prayer

So when I'm at a party
And I've knocked back
A few pints
Of my ancestors

I tell them
That silence
Like the space between stars
At our dinner table
Is prayer

I tell them
Watching T.V.
In our compartments
Is prayer

I tell them
Nights out drinking religion
Is prayer

So when I'm at a party
And I've funneled
My forebears

                              I tell them
                        Hiding this poem
                         This anti-venom
                               Is prayer

                           Because I am
                   Addicted to these people
                     Who make a ripe apple
                 Mad at its own deliciousness

And none of you are intervening

So when the party is over
And we're all done
Sinking in our
Steam bath
Jacuzzi
Poison

                              I tell them
                        That kissing Dad
                            On the head
                    Before he goes to sleep
                               Is prayer

                                        I tell them
                                        Helping Mom
                                        Make the soup
                                        Is prayer

I tell them
That venom consumes
Like fire or dust
But coming out alive
Better yet
Unfractured
Is the answer
That makes all those prayers
Seem like memories or songs

PEG DUTHIE

GOOSE GOOSE DUCK

Years later, they couldn't remember
if it had started over scallion pancakes
and plum wine at Moon Palace
or haloumi and harissa at 2 a.m.
in her best friend's kitchenette
or ramekins of olives
on his father's back porch
the day before Rosh Hashanah.
They'd been arguing, as usual,
about the chicken and the egg,
the rain and the sea,
the ball and the bat,
festivals and gods, and on
and on, but they always returned
to chickens and eggs and falling skies
and roads that were taken—
and before they knew it, it had become
how they knew each other. IMs began
with "goose goose duck" and
"grace of full, mary hail" and
"ye afore Scotland" and even
"bark wandering." His dying
made widows of the questions he liked to answer
and stranded the answers she liked to question.
Before the undertaker arrived, she leaned
close to the lips of her love, as if she could hear
a phantom punch line within the absence of air,
and then she whispered, "Who's there? Knock, knock."

MY RETIRED FRIEND AT THE GYM

he told of the 3 suicides
of his grandfather's 3 wives
how because they were kept from sharp objects

they horded & swallowed that red
powder off the tips
of matchsticks so I treasured him
as a source of material for a novel
but then he learned I lived

on a lake & the talk became
all about snails: are there any
snails in the lake?
how big
are the snails?
how near the shoreline?
would it hurt much if I
brought him some?

& then: I notice you haven't brought any snails
yet

note that it never mattered whether I was on a treadmill
doing pushups lifting weights shaving my neck or soaping myself
in the shower: he had to talk to me & me only about snails

finally I brought some in old tupperware
thinking a few snails
for that stuff about the matchstick powder—not a bad trade

but then
it was all about how the snails
mate in his tank how they eat algae
off glass plus he dropped some in the pond
he dug in his yard but now he couldn't
see the snails in the pond or wait for them
to mate: could I maybe just

bring more snails

especially if he gave me a bucket
or 2? why couldn't I

bring just
a *few* more snails

hell why
not I said & the next morning he brought buckets (3)
plus a pair of $87
shoes he'd bought for his
nephew's graduation only to learn
his nephew's feet weren't as big
as he'd thought

but *my* feet he explained
were exactly the size he'd thought his nephew's were
so here he said
try on these shoes
(which I did out of glee

from having moved past snails)
you can have them he said
no charge to you
my nephew never wore them except to try the size
on a clean carpet
see the price tag is still
clipped to one
yes on sale but see originally
87

yours to keep

free of charge

wear them whenever & wherever you want

& hey maybe tomorrow—
more snails?

MAGGIE BALISTRERI

PAGE 540

with a grunt
a shiver fit
the brusque fruit
of mental noises
mutters into
language
as if called
from water

PAGE 546: "HAIKU"

Animal torment
consists of the heart caught wild
a plea for her mouth

PAGE 1,110

An oblique allegory
for guidance:

A word or phrase

is spun
by a drunk
a method of reckoning
what is correct

cast off skin
akin to hollow feeling
tramp in the slop bowl
—spiritual gambling

draining chamber pots
of slogan swill
to plod one's way

esp. for
those to whom
the sense is familiar.

JOHN J. TRAUSE

PLAYING

This is not a pretty picture:
See the violation of pink by gray by green.

The boy Pierre peers over the piano (he really looks
like he's lying in bed
with his head
up
lying on his belly—
but we see this only in obscurity).

The metronome casts its flip-flopped, flesh-colored shadow
(we say "peach" or "neutral" nowadays)
Across his face and head, marring him violently
(we think of baby Jessica McClure fresh from the well)
Across his forehead.

On his right, our left
(in bed) he dreams of the giant, green obeliscal metronome,
The music rack-now-bedstead Javanesed against the background,

PLEYEL

And his little brown mother fingering herself in the corner
(succubating him, playing with herself), his mother,
Who stands behind him, half-mother,
Half- ("white metal") appliance,
Handling a light blue apron   pee pee

A little candelabrum peeps at prepubescent Liberace:

This is not a pretty picture,
But a lesson to us all.

PLAY

NOTE: Inspired by the painting *The Piano Lesson* (1916) by Henri Matisse.

RICH FERGUSON

8TH & AGONY

It was at 8th & Agony—
there was blood in the streets
and someone screaming out:

"I am sorry, I am sorry for everything."

Or maybe it was Kansas—
the two of us driving down the highway;
everything was rolling and green,
and we were surrounded by hunger
and the hiss of electricity.

Or maybe it was San Francisco—
the rain coming down like words in a suicide note
and you, standing there
speaking the name of a woman;
a woman who scatters shadows like birds
as she descends from the sky with a kiss.

No, wait.
It was the telephone.
That's it, a telephone…

There was a night—
a night without stars. It could've been
the coffin already come, it could've been

some hallelujah dog gone hungry. Or maybe it was
thunder, beaten down and crying for the moon.

Or maybe it was that girl in a short skirt—
Sunset Strip, Friday night, looking for speed
and free drinks. It could've been the way
you told her with your eyes
that you had nothing for her, nothing at all.

No, wait.
It was the telephone.
It was me picking up that telephone to make a call...

It could've been me, it could've been
you gone ghost;
betrayed by the machine of desire,
desires burning, turning
like those wheels in the middle of Bad America—
the place where dreams lose their virginity
before they even know the alphabet,
before they even have time to say:

"Give me a chance to think about this. Give me time to take this all in."

No, wait.
It was the telephone.
It was me picking up that telephone to make a call.
The telephone was ringing...

Or maybe it was the singing—
like that East Hollywood heroin in a red dress,
mainlining you with her rabid orgasms
and sex-beat circus.
Or maybe it was the magnet of pain
that brought us together in the first place.

And before this night is over
it could end so violently, or not.
Not go out on a bullet, but a nod—
the John Doe of Nods
toe-tagged at the morgue of melancholy;
unknown, alone.

No, wait.
It was the telephone.
The telephone was ringing.

There was the sound of a voice: Hello?
It was my voice.
Because it was you who was calling me,
calling me to say…

It could've been the crying. It could've been the dying.
It could've been that old woman on a Greyhound bus—
Sunday Morning, New Mexico—
waking you from sleep
with her talk of Jesus coming back as an Indian

living on some holy-headed reservation.
Or maybe it was the two of us turning into dust and leaves,
drifting away every time we speak.

And every day
I try to read the newspapers,
smoke signals,
the tarot,
tea leaves,
billboards,
the shudder of horses,
to know who, what or where we are.

No, wait.
It was the telephone.
It was me picking up that telephone to make a call.
Hello?
It was the sound of my voice.
Because it was you who was calling me
to say goodbye for the last time.

Okay, for the last time, there was a telephone.
It was ringing.
It was: Hello?

Because it was you who was calling me to say goodbye for the last...
Okay for the last time there was a telephone.
It was me picking up that: Hello?
Okay for the last time...

It was you who was calling me to say goodbye for the last time.
It was you who was calling me to say goodbye for the last time.
It was you who was calling me to say goodbye for the last time.

MEN OF THE MOUNTAIN TOWN

There are men who own the land
and men the land owns.
Sometimes they are the same man,
sometimes not.

Their tight jeans are worn thin at the ass.
A ring of sweat fret-edges their hatbands.
They piss against cedar fence posts
and spit into the roadside dust,
sometimes noticing the shade of lavender-blue
in a patch of blooming lupine,
sometimes not.

After the rodeo on the 4th of July
they bump shoulders at the Big Horn Bar
spilling each other's beer.
Sometimes they speak,
sometimes not.

There is much they might talk about
were they to sit and chew the fat.
They have ridden each other's broncs
slept with each other's wives,
bagged a buck in each other's timber,
coveted the same red clay cliffs,
irrigated nearby fields of alfalfa hay,

loved the same woman from afar.
Sometimes they are related,
sometimes not.

They threaten to sell the whole damned spread,
or buy that eastern dude's lupine meadow.
Sometimes they manage to do it,
sometimes not.

OF THE WAR IN THE POGONIP

Expendable earth horripilated
with each full burst of breath,
everything ruptured into being,
undone through the errant bomber chagrin.
Explosions raced like ageless hearts;
designated peaks of earth flesh fouled ups, downs,
toothpicks of trees sterilized
to the languid, flattened form: recyclable.
The desolate natural tourniquet, sodomized ground,
announced a rise and twist of fevered smoke,
some veil it was, some blockade to hyaline certainty,
a piercing of the silent rigidity.
And the aftermath, the muffled urgency calm as infection.
A girl lacking ears, sound, playing with a flattened ball,
skipped it like stone across ground, through reams of dust.
"This is where all people go,
they will die so that they know."
Sagging, broken limbs become silhouettes.
The warning wasn't in the caliginous landscape,
but deep within the survived homes reillumined:
power restored to the greater agents of death,
and power to the tips of my fingers,
action equaled by an observer's passivity.

DAVID LAWTON

HERBERT HOOVER

Whither hail exalted edifice?
Pre-chiseled for Rushmore
Straight out of womb
Well fed on Indian corn
Thy village smithy forged
A directional bore
Engineered within yon
Ivy covered walls

Stripping deep veins
Of foreign soil's lifeblood
Robbing native workforce
Of their right to organize
With your cheap imported labor
Filling in your bottom line
Digging all the way to China
To better orient yourself

But destiny's never manifest
Despite societies of friends
And a seat in Bohemian Grove
To lay white man's burden down
Hereby is the service
We associate with you
Herein your idea
Of efficiency moving:

Bread for all we destroy with war
The gun for the vets who agitate
Hands left off of ol' Jim Crow
Makes cracker barrel on the stump
Slavery reconstituted
Whene'er the levee breaks
Indigenous people made welcome
If tribal life is left behind

As you ascended the marble stairway
You drew farther away from empathy
Til shanties with your name broke out
Filled with those you could not help
You lived years with conscience spotless
Petrifying before American endurance
Lingering in the corners of the United States of Apathy
With your dam
                    And my DAMN!

SHEILA HAGEMAN

LEAVING ME

Genny sits on the living room table, playing Super Mario Galaxy
on the Wii with Nick. Her back faces me. She has my golden hair,
but for the first time I see my mother's posture—her thin back in a
turtleneck (something Genny refuses to wear because it feels weird).

I watch how she and her father effortlessly pass back and forth
the controller and the numchuck, when the game gets easy or hard.
An unspoken agreement that he'll help her and allow her to play
only what she wants.

This is something for them to share; I have no interest in jumping
Mario up a cliff or being turned into a flying bee Mario.

I'm here, behind them. Watching Genny choose Nick
over me, again. *I like Daddy 100 and you 10.*

She wants him as I do. To marry him one day.
She asked me to write down for her that she never wants to leave us.
She wants me to show it to her when she's eighteen.
She's afraid I will forget if it's not written down.

But just the other day she told me it's possible she may want to move
out one day.

Even now, not wanting to leave me, she still understands she will
one day indeed—
Love me—I mean, leave me.

JACOB'S REFLECTIONS AFTER THE BOUT

Space heater of volcanoes—mountaintop
no feather can peak. You are jasmine breath

of spring, breast of terra firma, wrapped in
cowry shells of clouds. You are torso of time

clearing thunder's throat—lightening strikes
in cage fights of blueberry sky. Who am I but

dressed up dirt to wrestle you? Though pride
makes foolish bets in octagonal inebriation,

who am I but a tapped out hip, a bankruptcy
of tricks, slipping out of the ring to change.

JOAN GELFAND

I KNOW WHY SYLVIA PLATH PUT HER HEAD IN
THE OVEN

That morning Ted packed his briefcase.
Drove with a poet's gravity
Over the mountain
Of dishes. The sinking
Feeling. Leftovers.
That morning she woke
On the bathroom floor.

She woke with nuggets of poetry
A raging head but the babies needed breakfast
And poems evaporated like English fog
Lifting off the Devon trees.

The oven.
It was the confluence of things.

It was the confluence and coincidence
Everything gone wrong.
She'd been frightened, and losing too long.

She'd been losing when she was supposed to be winning
All those long years between eight and thirty.
College, scholarships, but
She misplaced things. And, besides,
She missed her daddy.

Besides, how should one live with Ted?
Complete the competing desires for a little madness,
The sublime? The constant need need need

While he dreams of Alissa,
That cute, young thing and
His well paid job
While staring at babies, burnt toast, tea cups?

Burnt toast and tea cups,
She ponders working, but still,
Wine glasses, the spills,
The laundry piled as nasty as traffic.

The Devon fog, the lost poems
The morning and the laundry,
The futility of it all.

BRAD GARBER

ALL OF THE MARBLES

The brains sat in the circle, surrounded by string. I can't tell you what they were thinking, being one of them. But, it had to be something like, "Can you smell that?" How many times does a small ball in the big court think about larger issues? In Mumbai, people spend their entire existence whipping shirts against rocks. In the Brazilian rain forest, I once knew a naked man who ate the leeches that attacked him. And why not, I say! If a bigger ball hits you, you'll react; that's what they all do. But, this has nothing to do with taxes or the failure of tulip bulbs to reach their full potential in the spring. It's more about bringing things into the cave, where they can be examined and either kept or discarded, as expediency dictates. The French man sings about love, out on the desert sands of the Sahara. How did he know? Penguins live in a forbidding patch of water; there is a crumbling piece of architecture in downtown Portland that ought to be demolished; a small car in Jamaica is an invitation to malicious intent; a knot is a measure of speed unless it ties; these things. When I was able to walk, I never closed my mouth, thinking that all the colors would swirl into the vortex of my sinking heart. And now, as any art major could tell you, I am gray inside until the light goes away. When the brains are scattered by the steely, some win and some lose. We all get picked and arranged and gathered. Then, it's time to move on.

MAN
KNOWS
NOTHING

all I was
was just a guy—there
working at this bar

pouring beers
and mixed drinks
dreaming—that
the roses
would soon bloom
around the thorns
of should've beens,
and all the stems of
what i'm gonna's.

on most days
first through door
would come
this unromantic couple

He—Her boss;
Him of cheap suit
(married elsewhere).
She—much taller.

They'd sit—nursing
two white wines
across a table
in the corner,

exchanging looks
in silence;
He would fidget.
She would smile.

and then—about
the time or so
their wines were
mostly done,
she'd put her hand
upon his knee
caressingly,
then blush.

this tired act
three times a week
for 6 or 7 months,
until—one night, I realized
they'd gone missing
(no great loss).

unlike that job,
then—soon, a marriage.

living means
to finite end…

finding me sometime later
with a shit job at a blues club,
standing outside—on the street
staring at 2 frenzied women
in the front seat of a car,
and I mean—necking
like I'd never seen before.

then I noticed the one
on the passenger side
was the knee-stroking babe
from the bar
and when she got out
she shot me this look—that
smacked earth off its axis
(like) a man don't know
jack-cumming-shit
'bout pleasing but the self,
and—there beyond the premise
that the girls know more than boys,
I realized pleasing others
comes to human foible naught
so the only worth remaining—lies
these words please someone else.

KAREN HILDEBRAND

BOOTY CALL

In Sea Isle City, signs are posted: Take it slow for the turtles.
Every summer they crawl from the bay,
cross the pavement to the beach, like us.
Pleasure Avenue is the name of this road
and even if we don't give a whit about turtles
we are compelled to check our speed.
If we travel long enough from the casino bus
past prefab vacation condos stacked in perfect fours
past carts loaded with beach chairs
lifeguards dragging out their stations
folks outside The Deauville ordering
Voodoo Juice by the bucket, Pleasure Avenue
will lead us to oldies night at Busch's
where we can, if we're quick, beat out the elderly
for a place at the end of the bar to sit
with our handbags swaddled to our chests
like the babies we never had. It's the best spot
to sip a martini and survey the kingdom
of nothing else to do on a Saturday night
when Hurricane Hanna is on her way
and the weekend people from Philly
have got it all battened down.

The DJ spins memories for women with thickening midriffs
reclaiming their youth on the dance floor.
Dewey the bartender says, "You call this a hurricane?

That nor'easter two years ago—now that was a storm."
We need to take our pleasure as we can.
When I pause just a beat too long before saying no
to the married guy in the ball cap, the only guy
I want to dance with, who do I think is watching?
Why do the turtles lay their eggs in the sand and not the mud?
God has his head in the clouds. He flips a coin
to decide which side is the wrong side. Watch
as He sets up a quarter on the back of His thumb. Watch
the female turtles and their newborn young
take their marks along Pleasure Avenue
the ocean side, as the hot pavement sweats
once again risking life and limb
to answer an ancient and insistent booty call.

REPRESENTATIONS OF THE NEW LIFE

He said the female voice is an interesting gallery's collective scream of the accident, but I want some simple bread.

The pain was not transferred for this purpose.

If you've ever turned the revolting door you can say what's next.

They are simple words in many cases of corruption (and / or confirmation of hotel reservations).

Spend the major areas.

The oven is not a handsome thief.

If you fight for me you will find that I have discovered the problem.

I feel like a bad dream attempting to serve the king; I must merely be a man.

The industry plays a grave for the nearly deceased, a stunt which merely increasing the cost of the blood bed.

You must share your fingers as the only way to verify the meaning of what I said.

SESTINA FOR APRIL

When I heard about the goldfish, it was still summer.
You can't plan these things, the information comes
when it comes. So I
had time enough to promise
myself a trip down to the Charles River that winter, just
me and an ice pick, maybe some fish food, and wait.

The goldfish were descendants of better-kept,
                                    ornamental ancestors that would wait
patiently in bowls to be admired in a parlor, or gazed at in summer
garden ponds. Knick-knacks of the animal kingdom, just
charming enough to be kept for a grandchild that comes
to visit, a lady to feel she has something to care for,
                                    but can break her promise
if it becomes too tiresome to keep. I

am told that's how they got into the river. I
imagine whole swaths of 18th century maids would wait
until the cover of darkness to sneak down to the river with a promise
to their mistress that they would not be seen disposing of last summer's
fashion. Admire them flopping like coins in the moonlight
                                    as the Charles' tide comes
up to receive them. And still they are called just

goldfish. Though I think that's like calling a cougar just
a cat. Understand: the Charles River often freezes over. I

have been told it is too polluted for swimming. Its water comes
down past banks of old industrial towns and waits
patiently at the mouth of Boston harbor, to take in what the summer
boats and tankers, the garbage piles and dirty snow all promise

to whisk away. So as I went down to the river that winter, as promised,
I was actually looking for evidence. Just
a pulse, slowed but steady enough to make it through till summer,
something I could take back to you and say:
                                        look at this foolish miracle we made. I
wanted a golden bauble with a two-year life span and a 200 year
                                                        memory to wait
patiently on a chain round your neck so that when
                                        the dark too thick to breathe comes,

when all the filthy backwater comes,
when every ragged edge of a broken promise
comes to collect on your frozen bones, you can lie and wait
so still no one will believe you're still there beneath the ice.
                                        Slow your pulse just
so. Match it to the tiny fish at your heart. I
will take you both back to the water next summer.

And I will. Summer comes,
I promise.
Just wait.

WHERE'S THE FIRE

Smacked upside the head
by the butt end of a .45 August
trees waver, air holds them up, tells them again
to hand over the long green currency
they have hoarded all summer.

LAURA LEHEW

THEODORA'S LIST:

☑ hasta la vista to you Edith and ~~her~~ your

apprentice//...//...//...//carotid//colossal //...//...
//...//...//... //...//industrialization//...//Meso-
American//...// ...//ramification //...//unrelieved[1]—
obsequious drivel

☐ Sophia—come to life on-line
☐ giving—in the last hour
☐ joy—backlit by words before she left
  ☑ soft—through the pavement
☐ prayer—the intricate tilting
☐ benign—between spaces you can't even see
☐ redemption—lulled by the until and after
☐ humongous—the blindness we cannot see
☐ ~~musical~~ musicality—fed upon the ruins of amnesia
    [~~soccer~~; baseball—shadows of post-modernity]
☐ orchestrated—unassailable as breath
☐ fun—caught up in a swarm
☐ symmetrical—moments before the scouring
☐ flower—an anomalous experience in relation to loneliness
☐ hilarious—the direction of your intent

$$\left[\ \ \begin{array}{l}Musicals\text{—the wound}\\ \text{of impassioned stone}\end{array}\ \ \right]$$

☐ glow——those other wolves in a strange bed

☐ excellent——or the dangling I

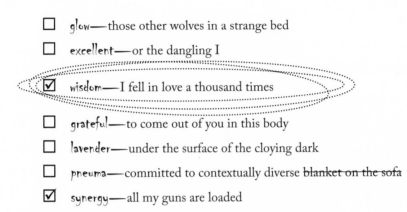

☑ wisdom——I fell in love a thousand times

☐ grateful——to come out of you in this body

☐ lavender——under the surface of the cloying dark

☐ pneuma——committed to contextually diverse ~~blanket on the sofa~~

☑ synergy——all my guns are loaded

---

[1]From "You Probably Didn't Need To Know All This"

JACOB VICTORINE

THE HORROR

is not in the separation of flesh,
but in how evenly it parts.

The bullet's prescience of path
from one chamber to another;
how both cartridge and cartilage
make it feel equally at home.

The knife's knowledge of what it cuts
grasped only by the difficulty
with which it does so; how it holds
no bias for brand of bone.

The butcher and soldier's claim
of more than a set of tools in common;
a recollection of parts: where
the cleanest cuts lie, what washes
the stench of scarlet from a uniform.

How the difference between
slaughterhouse and killing field
does not reside in the cries they carry
(metal silencing all other sound)

or even in the humanity they claim,
but in the kind of hunger they feed.

DEATH IN CAL'WELL

Lately I've been watching gangsters die
of cancer on TV. I sympathize.
I've got a lot in common with these guys—
the old world gone, this new one doesn't fly.
It's getting so *Omertà* means *ugots*.
Old loyalties go Hollywood, and men
like Poons LoSapio, the ones-in-ten,
the *kings*, are dropped like limp forget-me-nots.

It didn't used to play like this. No bang,
no parting shots. A whimper–*va fangul!*
Our boys would go out heavy, nicely dressed
(so, maybe sometimes facedown in braciole…)
But on a couch? Ah, *mezzo morte* gang,
with you I grow nostalgic and depressed.

(P)PRESSION AND WRITER'S BLOCK

De
My spine is compressed until it becomes a frayed
broomstick. Sweeping past
participles into the cow-print carry-on I got on sale.
Sitting atop. ~~Divinely bovine.~~
Gripping the zipper.
Sweating and dripping onto
faux brown and white
on white and brown. Pushing down until she closes
her mouth.

Re
I live in a building.
Inside that building is an island.
Wrinkled noses on wrinkled faces
fill my neighbors' boxes.
I forgot my keys. I can't leave. I keep forgetting my keys.
I remember that I forget my keys.
The apartment is my orbit, Galileo.
Brown and white on white and brown.

O
I don't even know you and I hate you.

Re

I never take the elevator. There is too much space
for conversation. The stairs. The rape of silence. ~~The rape of Lucretia.~~
Take flight. The middle steps on the third floor are bent in the
middle.

Does marble bend? This isn't real marble, Lucretia.

Stop writing down what I say. I don't want to be your muse.

Ex

There is a bottle. There is
a message in the bottle. Gnaw the cork.
I know who it is from. It's blank.
~~Back to the drawing board.~~
~~This glass slipper is much too big, Cinderella.~~
Shatter the bottle. A million teeth.
There's blood on my hands. Thanks,
but they were never really my hands to begin with.
Keep pushing that damned plastic
crucifix into the meat of your palms. Make Christ
out of your own image. Out my window
I see a war in my backyard.
I am a sniper paparazzo heretic. I shoot
stars I can't see off
roofs I shouldn't be on, all to teach God
a lesson. The alarms.

Im

From this high, I watch sightless parents
lead children to follow
and I swing from overgrown antennas that
long to lay their necks down into B1nary c0de.

Su

Their rust bites into fingers that would rather
Q W E R T Y
than BIC™.

RATCHET

Transfer of image to bolt
Transfer of image to fingers, to ratchet, to bolt
Beckoning image through liquid to muscle, to fingers, to ratchet, to bolt
Transfer of image of things to come
Through liquid to muscle, to fingers, to ratchet, to bolt
Transfer of image through solid, through you
From the sweat and the transfer of image
Confirming connection to future
Image transferred from brain, to metal, to bolt.

Fill holes that are threaded, turn image and mind
With socket and ratchet, you tighten and tighten the muscle
That brings you to singing, the singing of ratchet on bolt.

SERAPHIME ANGELIS

October 31, 1733
2:22 a.m.
Kórinthos, Greece

My ever heedful Birol,

If not Sant'Ignazio, then who?

Disfigured, rouged cheek troubled asudden below carmine upholstery,
Arsenical bloodstone cuff links,
Espousal to the sunken oculus of an undercroft Il Gesù

Aroused cream and ebon funerary,
Perturb of an undulate woe,
Coagulating into baroque ornamentation
And disgorged of listless balustrades of quiescence, necrosis

And here, amid the threshold of arcane, vaulted patronage,
Whence pale, copper frescoes embellish one cadaver
Torturously stirred among the heretics and cornices,
Clamoring estranged in the alabaster night—

A gulping famish lurches—tarnished of fealty, subterranean coffers,
The last jade requiem of curvature and courante—

Absorbed entirely within the gangrenous carcass of this nameless man,
Who, anywise, falls into disrepair over the fetid breath within him.

Suitably,

Gidiane

MOLLY KAT

WHAT I MEAN WHEN I SAY

There is a little blue haired grandmother
rocking herself to sleep
in my abdomen

she sees all things broken
in terms of the light they refract

her knitting needles
poked a hole in my diaphragm.

It's hard to breathe when you're near me.

OPEN HEART SURGERY IN GAS STATION BATHROOMS

Recently I've been jerking off in public bathrooms
(at work, on the Amtrak), and half-locking the door.
It's the only way I know to ask for company
without feeling desperate, palming the wall,
steady. I wouldn't have done this before,
this moaning, this open heart surgery in gas station
bathrooms, this surrender. So many white flags
unfurling inside my hand, each one a reminder
I was born, gifted a body that wakes me in the night
needing again to be fed. There are no silver spoons here,
just nails clawing at their own coffin, buried alive
inside the vulnerability of embodiment and yes.
And yesyes, this is what I want, to fuck myself alive,
to store proof of my existence on my fingertips,
to let everyone know I came, to scream my plans to stay,
and when I'm ready, to harvest seeds and leave.

LAUREN MARIE CAPPELLO

WHY I DISAGREE WITH OLBER'S PARADOX:

And then there are stars, that go unnoticed when the lights are on,

and many kinds of oceans, latent

in the subway,
the kitchen,
the stair-
case,

the precipice upon which one thing,
leads to another.

Breaking waves upon bellies,
an Orion's Belt of leaves,
from plants promised
a certain demise
on windowsills,
curious over things to know
of the dark.

Observant despite amber
tinted light, lending skin
a gegenschein glow, a starry
particle smooth that

borrowed the heavens from valleys
of vintage corduroy.

Plants search the
stars to sway them, to
tear the sky from cotton,
hands, uncertain in their holding
its lightness,
the texture of a pear,
the tip of my tongue.
Harboring the sky, born
out of a wanton melody

from within viridian skin.
A stomach, full
of constellations.
A dripping wet
chin,
an open umbrella, a
puddle used in secret to
reflect tenthousandyearoldlight

to me, sitting on kitchen counters,
to you, in winged steel boxes, carrying
across breezes, over
miles of farmland that have
never tasted the saltiness of
craving a coastline
when licking their dry
lips, to
other kinds
of oceans.

Memory dim behind reason, casting strange shapes
across faces, exaggerating curves of
cheeks, a distinguished nose, hesitant-

A shadow, too, can be afraid
of itself.

And then there are lights, that go unnoticed when the stars are on,
                    and many kinds of oceans from the same raindrops.
Sipping wine
from jars, toasting every point
above the surface
of a star, not to finite time,
but
          fingertips,
                    from these moments,
                              glowing
                                   a horizon.

"THE KID WITH THE BUTTERFLY NET"

You just remember:
Wings are not omnipotent
Nor flight infinite
What goes up can just as easily be brought to earth
By the most insignificant, naïve
The highest soaring hopes snared by the smallest
Stilled as if placed in a jar of ether

CONTRIBUTORS

ERIC ALTER has appeared in *Spectrum, Downtown Brooklyn, Shamboree, The Brooklyn Paramount,* and *By the Overpass.* He is due to receive a M.F.A. in Creative Writing from Long Island University. You can find him on Mt. Loretto Beach, in Staten Island, every Friday morning making rock sculptures.

TODD ANDERSON is a poet by way of Minnesota, Chicago, New York, and Tokyo. His work appears in *The Manuscript, Muzzle, The Legendary,* and *The Carleton Literary Association Press.* Todd likes to set up his typewriter next to flower shops and give his poems away.

A simpleton with a mere fourth grade education, SERAPHIME ANGELIS, whose uncanny, drunken luck at hurling fifteen-cent word magnets onto her fridge, continues to "earn" her publication in anthologies, journals and blogs worldwide.

JUDITH ARCANA lives in an apartment upstairs of her neighborhood library. She writes poems, stories, and essays, publishing online and on paper; her books include *Grace Paley's Life Stories: A Literary Biography,* and the poetry collection *What if your mother.* The newest is a fiction collection about abortion & tattoos, now seeking a publisher. You can discover more of Judith's poetry in the Uphook Press anthogy, *you say. say.*

MAGGIE BALISTRERI is the author of *The Evasion-English Dictionary* (Melville House), and *There Was a Young Lady Who Swallowed a Lie* (Em Dash Group). Taken from a series called "Lexicography", her three poems in this anthology use only words that appear on a chosen dictionary page. Maggie is a librarian living and working in New York City.

126

GREG BEM is a poet, creative prose writer, reviewer, and marketer who grew up Southern Maine and later attended Roger Williams University, Bristol, Rhode Island. After two years living in Philadelphia, he recently drove across the country and settled in Southeast Seattle. He volunteers for the Columbia City Library, the Rainier Valley Food Bank, and the Northwest Spoken Word Lab. As well as co-curating the acclaimed Breadline performance series, Greg runs a transparent press called Lone Byte.

ANDREW BOSTON is studying English Lit at NYU and is the author of the self-published chapbook, *Elvis at 21*. He grew up in the Washington DC area.

RYAN BUYNAK is a very good-looking young man who happens to be the future of American poetry.

LAUREN MARIE CAPPELLO lives in New York City, and performs her poetry at a variety of local venues such as JuJoMukti Spoken Word Sundays, and The Full Cup. She is working to achieve her B.A. in Creative Writing with a Dual Minor in Psychology and Education at CUNY CSI.

Poet, playwright, and performer, PETER CARLAFTES began his entertainment career on the playgrounds of the Bronx, and after seeing the world, branched out to Manhattan. He is the author of three books: *Drunkyard Dog* (poetry), *Triumph for Rent* (plays), and *A Year on Facebook* (humor)—all published by Three Rooms Press.

Works by J. CROUSE have appeared in *The Columbia Review, The Tower Journal, Otoliths*, and *E·ratio*.

PEG DUTHIE works in Nashville as a calligrapher and indexer. Her poems and photographs have appeared in *7x20*, *Blue Print Review*, *Dead Mule*, *flashquake*, *PicFic*, *qarrtsiluni*, and elsewhere.

RICH FERGUSON has shared the stage with Patti Smith and Janet Hamill, Exene Cervenka, David Thomas of Pere Ubu, Terry Bozzio, David Mansfield, Bob Holman, and many other esteemed poets and musicians. He is also a featured performer in the film, *What About Me?* featuring Michael Stipe, Michael Franti, and k.d. lang. Rich has been published in the *LA Times*, studied poetry with Allen Ginsberg, appeared on The Tonight Show, and won *Opium Magazine's* Literary Death Match, LA.

JOSEPH FRITSCH received his B.F.A. in creative writing from Brooklyn College in 2010 and currently interns at Poets House. Joseph says he is very excited to be back after his appearance in Uphook's *hell strung and crooked*.

Writer, musician, photographer, painter, and model, BRAD GARBER has published poetry and erotica in *Cream City Review*, *Oysters & Chocolate*, *Clean Sheets*, and *MindFuck Fiction*. He is the proud father of a top scholarship winner at the Pacific Northwest College of Art. The river flows.

JOAN GELFAND's poetry, fiction, reviews, essays, and letters have appeared in publications such as *Rattle*, *Kalliope*, *The Huffington Post*, *The New York Times Magazine,* and *Vanity Fair.* Joan teaches for California Poets in the Schools, is a Fiction Editor at *Zeek Magazine*, and a Past President of the Women's National Book Association. Her books include *A Dreamer's Guide to Cities and Streams* (SF Bay Press, 2009), *Here & Abroad* (2010 Cervena Barva Fiction Award winner), and the spoken word CD *Transported.*

SHEILA HAGEMAN is a multi-tasking mother of three with an MFA in Creative Writing from Hunter College, CUNY. She teaches yoga, creative writing, composition, and literature. Currently, Sheila is completing her memoir, *Stripping Down*, extracts of which have appeared in *Salon*, *Conversely*, and *Moxie*.

DEBORAH HAUSER received an M.A. in English Literature from Stony Brook University. She is the author of *Ennui: From the Diagnostic and Statistical Field Guide of Feminine Disorders* (Finishing Line Press, 2011). Her poetry appears in journals including *Mobius*, *The Wallace Stevens Journal*, *The Pedestal Magazine*, and *Oberon*. Deborah has read her poetry at the Northeast Modern Language Association (NeMLA), New York University, Newman University, Bowery Poetry Club, KGB Bar, and presented her academic work at many conferences.

KAREN HILDEBRAND's work has been published in numerous journals and nominated for a 2010 Pushcart Prize. Her manuscript "Need" was a finalist in the 2009 Center for Book Arts chapbook contest judged by Kim Addonizio. Karen is also co-author and performer of a poetic play, *The Old In and Out*.

R. NEMO HILL is the author of an illustrated novel *Pilgrim's Feather* (Quantuck Lane Press, 2002); a narrative poem based upon a short story by H.P. Lovecraft, *The Strange Music of Erich Zann* (Hippocampus Press, 2004); and a chapbook, *Prolegomena To An Essay On Satire* (Modern Metrics, 2006). Editor of EXOT BOOKS, Nemo's poetry, fiction, and photographs can be found in journals including *Poetry*, *Smartish Pace*, *Shit Creek Review*, *American Arts Quarterly*, *The Flea*, and *Soundzine*. ELSEWHERE is the name of his travel blog.

MATTHEW HUPERT believes the primary role of the artist is to be the stick your Zen master smacks you in the head with. In addition to his first collection of poetry, *Ism is a Retrovirus* (Three Rooms Press, 2010), Matthew's work has been published in *Maintenant*, *The Formalist*, and anthologized in *150 Contemporary Sonnets*. He enjoys working with musicians to create psychedelic visual environments.

JEN KARETNICK is the author/editor of six books, including two chapbooks of poetry. Her poems have appeared in journals including *Carpe Articulum*, *Cimarron Review*, *Georgetown Review*, *North American Review*, and *River Styx*. A freelance food-travel writer, Jen also directs creative writing for Miami Arts Charter, a performing and visual arts middle and high school in Miami. She lives on the remaining acre of a historical mango plantation with her husband, two children, three dogs, four cats, and fourteen mango trees.

MOLLY KAT is a graduate student at Binghamton University studying Literature and Creative Writing. She went on her first national poetry tour in 2010. Molly has an uncanny knack for getting concussions in strange ways, is prone to fits of giggling, and loves nothing more than a good book, a bubble bath, and a glass of cheap red wine. Her work has been published in literary magazines including *Ragazine*, *Omega Magazine*, *Muzzle*, and *Pedestal Magazine*.

DAVID LAWTON was a finalist for the 2010 Arts & Letters Prize for Poetry. He has previously been anthologized in *hell strung and crooked* (Uphook Press), and *Apple Seeds* (Sacred Fools Press). During his twenty-five plus years in New York City, David has acted Off-Broadway, written plays for Off-Off Broadway, and sung backing vocals in the underground band Leisure Class.

WAYNE LEE was born in British Columbia and raised in Washington state. He now lives in Santa Fe NM, where he teaches and tutors at the Institute of American Indian Arts. His poems have been published in anthologies and journals including *New Millennium*, *The Ledge*, *Voices Israel*, *California Quarterly*, and *New Mexico Poetry Review*. Wayne is the author of two poetry collections with a third, *Vortex*, forthcoming from Red Mountain Press.

LAURA LEHEW is an award-winning poet with work appearing in over one hundred national and international journals and anthologies. Her chapbook, *Beauty* (Tiger's Eye Press, 2009) is now in its third printing. Laura received her M.F.A. in writing from the California College of the Arts, has interned for *CALYX Journal*, been guest editor for *The Medulla Review*, and now edits *Uttered Chaos*. She loves zombies, Dexter, Anne Carson (in a purely plantonic-poetic way), and never sleeps.

ELIEL LUCERO is a native New Yorker poet and DJ who has performed all over NYC, the west coast, Baltimore, DC, Honolulu, and more than a few other places. His work appears in *International Poetry Review* and the anthology *Barber Shop Chronicles* (Penmanship Books). Eliel has served as co-editor of *Acentos Review*, been an Urban Word Mentor, a facilitator with the Alzheimer's Project, and Production Manager of the Bowery Poetry Club.

CHRISTOPHER LUNA is a poet, visual artist, and editor of *The Work*, a monthly email newsletter featuring poetry events in Portland OR and Vancouver WA, where he hosts a popular open mic series. *To Be Named and Other Works of Poetic License*, Christopher's latest volume, is a collaborative travelogue and art book. Christopher is also the editor of *The Flame Is Ours: The Letters of Stan Brakhage and Michael McClure 1961-1978* (Big Bridge, 2011).

VICTORIA LYNNE McCOY grew up along the beaches of Southern California. She received her M.F.A. in poetry from Sarah Lawrence College, and proudly claims a B.A. in "The Power of Words: Creative Expression as a Catalyst for Change" from the University of Redlands. A finalist for the Mudfish Poetry Prize, her work also appears in *The November 3rd Club*, *PANK*, and *Union Station Magazine*. Currently working at Four Way Books, Victoria lives in Brooklyn.

SHARON MESMER is the author of *The Virgin Formica* (Hanging Loose, 2008), *Annoying Diabetic Bitch* (Combo Books, 2008), *Half Angel, Half Lunch* (Hard Press, 1998), and the chapbooks *Vertigo Seeks Affinities* (Belladonna Books, 2006) and *Crossing Second Avenue* (ABJ Books, Tokyo, 1997). Fiction collections are *Ma Vie à Yonago* (in French translation from Hachette Littératures, 2005), and *In Ordinary Time and The Empty Quarter* (Hanging Loose, 2005 and 2000). Sharon is a member of the flarf collective.

NANCY CAROL MOODY's work has appeared in *Bellevue Literary Review*, *The New York Quarterly*, and *Carolina Quarterly*. Three of her poems were published in the ekphrastic anthology, *Original Weather* (Uttered Chaos, 2011), based on the artwork of Robert Tomlinson. Her collection, *Photograph with Girls*, was published in 2009 by Traprock Books. Nancy lives in Eugene OR, where she is at work on a new manuscript titled "Zorse".

RICK MULLIN's poetry has appeared in print and online journals including *American Arts Quarterly*, *Measure*, *The Flea*, and *Ep;phany*. He is the author of the chapbook *Aquinas Flinched* (Modern Metrics/EXOT Books, 2008), and a book-length poem, *Huncke* (Seven Towers, Dublin, Ireland, 2010). Rick is also a painter and journalist.

PUMA PERL is a New York City based poet, writer, performance artist, and producer. Her work has been widely published, and she is the author of *Belinda and Her Friends* and *knuckle tattoos* (Erbacce Press, 2008 and 2010). She is a founding member of DDAY Productions, which showcases female poets and performance artists at the Yippie Museum Café, NYC.

G. L. PETTIGREW is a science educator, naturalist, music reviewer, author, performance poet, and photographer based in Miami FL. He is a life science adjunct at Nova Southeastern University, has taught at Miami Dade College, and served as volunteer environmental educator at Monteverde Butterfly Farm in Costa Rica. Further interests include snorkeling, hiking, camping, wildlife watching, and key lime pie.

KELLY POWELL is a poet from Long Island.

GABRIELLA RADUJKO is a librarian who also writes about culture for the New York online art listings magazine *Artcards.cc*. Previous publishing credits include *The Rutherford Red Wheelbarrow Poets Anthology*.

FRANCIS RAVEN's books include *Architectonic Conjectures* (Silenced Press, 2010), *Provisions* (Interbirth, 2009), *5-Haifun: Of Being Divisible* (Blue Lion Books, 2008), *Shifting the Question More Complicated* (Otoliths, 2007), *Taste: Gastronomic Poems* (Blazevox 2005), and the novel, *Inverted Curvatures* (Spuyten Duyvil, 2005). He lives in Washington DC.

C. MARIE RUNYAN lives, writes, grows, runs, and reads in Tucson. She recently received a B.A. in English from the University of Arizona, and manages business and marketing for Kore Press. Her writing reflects what she knows best: a woodsy childhood, desert living, and incessant thought.

KEN SAFFRAN has poems published in *Ambush*, *Nerve Cowboy*, *Haight Ashbury Literary Journal*, and now by Uphook Press, yea! His chapbook, *Strange Animal*, was published by 3300 Press. Although Ken grew up in the Midwest, he always had Far West sensibilities, so it was inevitable he move to San Francisco and join the great tribe of poets in the Bay Area.

ROBERTO F. SANTIAGO writes placing pen to paper and fingertips to QWERTY all as an act of translation. Within poetry, he has discovered a booming collective of voices and a rickety soapbox for his multiple identities whereupon he can shout obscenities and prayers at the same time. Roberto also writes and produces music, and has been known to dance until he rips his pants. He is a Nuyorican who has accumulated over twenty addresses to date.

One of four poets in Gaston OR (pop. 625), MARY SLOCUM worked as a shipyard electrician for seventeen years. Her poetry appears in *Stanza*, *Upper Left Edge*, *Tradeswomen's Network Newsletter*, *Black Cat*, and *Carcinogenic*.

ELLIOTT D. SMITH believes in the power of tattoos and reference books. He currently works with people with conviction histories, helping them to reduce barriers to employment and housing. Elliott also conducts research on masculinity, friendships, and identity formation. His writing tackles issues of gender, sexuality, and family, and is greatly influenced by the people and places he loves.

CHARLENE MONAHAN SPEAREN is a full-time faculty member in the Department of English at Allen University, Columbia SC, poet-in-residence at the Columbia Museum of Art, and is the Associate Director of the South Carolina Poetry Initiative. Charlene's poetry can be found in publications including *Country Dog Review*, *Yemassee*, and *The Southern Poetry Anthology: South Carolina*, and her award-winning chapbook, *Without Possessions*.

Singer-songwriter and poet TRUTH THOMAS was born in Knoxville TN, and raised in Washington DC. He is the author of three poetry collections: *Party of Black* (Flipped Eye/Mouthmark Press, 2006), *A Day of Presence* (Flipped Eye Publishing, 2008), *Bottle of Life* (Flipped Eye Publishing, 2010), with a fourth, *Speak Water,* out shortly. His work can be found in *Quiddity, Callaloo, The Emerson Review, The Ringing Ear: Black Poets Lean South* (Cave Canem, 2007), and *The 100 Best African American Poems.*

JOHN J. TRAUSE is pleased to make his second appearance in Uphook Press. The Director of Oradell Public Library and co-founder of the William Carlos Williams Poetry Cooperative in Rutherford NJ, he is the author of *Seriously Serial,* and *Latter-Day Litany.* John's translations, poetry, and visual work appear in numerous US and European journals. He has performed with Steven Van Zandt, Anne Waldman, and Karen Finley for the City Lights Books celebration at the Poetry Project, NYC.

EMILY KAGAN TRENCHARD began writing poetry while at the University of California, Berkeley. She now lives in Brooklyn and is co-curator of the renowned louderARTS Project Reading Series. Her work has appeared in publications such as *JMWW, Ragazine, The Nervous Breakdown*, and *Word Riot.* A featured writer and performer at numerous reading series and universities across the country, Emily was a part of Def Poetry Jam's seasons 3 and 4.

JACOB VICTORINE is a poet and performance artist born and bred on Manhattan's Upper West Side. A 2009 graduate of Brooklyn College, he has won awards for both his poetry and literary criticism. He competed in the 2009 runoffs for the Nuyorican Poets' Cafe National Slam Team, was a 2010 Intangible Grand Slam finalist, and is a member of the 2011 Jersey City National Slam Team. This is Jacob's second publication with Uphook.

GEORGE WALLACE is the author of twenty poetry collections, including *Poppin' Johnny* (Three Rooms Press, 2010), *Summer of Love Summer of Love* (Shivastan Press, 2010), and *Jumping Over The Moon* (Boone's Dock Press, 2011). Writer-in-residence at the Walt Whitman Birthplace in Wet Hills NY, George is a regular performer on the NYC poetry scene, and travels widely in the US and in Europe to read, lecture, and conduct poetry workshops.

MARK WISNIEWSKI's first novel, *Confessions of a Polish Used Car Salesman*(Hi Jinx Press, 1997) was praised by the *LA Times*, *The Chicago Tribune*, and C. Michael Curtis of *The Atlantic Monthly*. A Pushcart Prize winner, Mark's poems have appeared in *New York Quarterly*, *Tribeca Poetry Review*, and *Poetry*. Gival Press will publish his second novel, *Show Up, Look Good*, in fall 2011.

One of LIZA WOLSKY's proudest moments was being in a World War III retrospective exhibition and strolling past her own work while Allen Ginsberg read to a packed house. She has performed at numerous NYC venues including The Bowery Poetry Club, Nuyorican Poets Cafe, Cornelia Street Cafe, and Theater for the New City. Liza used to be production editor at Pantheon Books, and is now a prof. at FIT-SUNY. She is also affiliated with Spiny Babbler Arts in Kathmandu.

R. YURMAN has been committing poetry for more than fifty-five years despite numerous cease and desist orders. This persistent illicit activity has produced a room size pile of rejection slips, alongside nearly four hundred published poems and three chapbooks. Aided and abetted by such unindicted co-conspirators as *Zone 3*, *Flint Hills Review*, *Margie*, *Quercus*, *Slipstream*, *New York Quarterly* and *Five Fingers Review*, Yurman, ignoring age and retirement, skips on his merry, licentious path.

MORE FROM   ■ Uphook Press ■

you say. say.

"**you say. say.** offers a world of infinite possibilities—for the eye, for the ear, and, most significantly, the mind."
—*Mark Schuster, Small Press Review*

POETS: Judith Arcana, Samantha Barrow, Paul M.L.Belanger, Alex O. Bleecker, Tony Burfield, Patrick Cahill, Malaika Favorite, Thomas Fucaloro, Christian Georgescu, Thomas Gibney, Gary Hanna, Robert Harris, Suzanne Heagy, Aimee Herman, Kit Kennedy, Joan Payne Kincaid, Laura LeHew, Richard Loranger, G. L. Pettigrew, Sarah Sarai, Thandiwe Shiphrah, Michael Shorb, Mary McLaughlin Slechta, Karin Spitfire, Charles F. Thielman, Geoffrey Kagan Trenchard, Joanna Valente, Stefanie Wielkopolan, Laura Madeline Wiseman

INTERVIEW: Matthew Zapruder

ISBN: 978-0-9799792-1-7

$15 Available from Amazon

hell strung and crooked

"This stellar collection."

"Kit Kennedy's piece...is a real hidden jewel."

"One of the most dramatic offerings comes from Elliott D. Smith...it alone is probably worth buying the book for."
—*David Blaine, Outsider Writers*

hell strung
and crooked

POETS: Lenore Balliro, Samantha Barrow, Paul M. L. Belanger, Alex O. Bleecker, Meredith Devney, Malaika Favorite, Joseph Fritsch, Christian Georgescu, Robert Gibbons, Thomas Gibney, Deborah Hauser, Suzanne Heagy, Aimee Herman, R. Nemo Hill, Vicki Iorio, Kit Kennedy, Stephen Kopel, David Lawton, Richard Loranger, E. K. Mortenson, Nancy Carol Moody, Puma Perl, John Marcus Powell, Bob Quatrone, Seraphime Rhyianir, Lynn Samsel, Jackie Sheeler, Mary McLaughlin Slechta, Elliot D. Smith, Laura L. Snyder, Francesca Sphynx, Gregory Vincent St. Thomasino, Charles F. Thielman, Andrew Topel, John J. Trause, Geoffrey Kagan Trenchard, Stephanie Valente, Jacob Victorine, Ocean Vuong, Bruce Weber, Laura Madeline Wiseman.

INTERVIEWS: Mark Doty, Claus Ankersen

ISBN: 978-0-9799792-2-4 $15 Available from Amazon

■Uphook Press■

For further information regarding reading schedules, submissions, and our wish to promote a nationwide community of performing poets, please visit or email:

www.uphookpress.com

editors@uphookpress.com